RICK BRYANT

Explore San Francisco

Top Attractions, Best Restaurants, Beaches, Hikes,
Sights, and Much More

This book was professionally typeset on Reedsy.
Find out more at reedsy.com

To my thoughtful and loving Mom SGK, who grew up in San Francisco
I Love you, Rick

There's no time to be bored in a city as beautiful as San Francisco~ Unknown

Contents

Preface

Having lived in San Francisco when I was younger, was a truly enriching experience filled with unforgettable memories and endless exploration. From the iconic sights of the Golden Gate Bridge and Beaches to the vibrant neighborhoods like Chinatown and the Mission District, every corner of this city offers a unique blend of culture, history, and natural beauty. Whether it was strolling through the bustling streets of Fisherman's Wharf, savoring the diverse culinary delights, or soaking in the breathtaking views from Twin Peaks, San Francisco never ceased to amaze me. I've poured my heart and soul into this travel guide, sharing my favorite spots and hidden gems, hoping to inspire you to discover the wonders, adventure, and undeniable charm that await you in this captivating city by the bay. Thank you for joining me on this journey—I hope you find as much joy in exploring San Francisco as I did.

1

Chapter 1. Explore San Francisco

Thank you for choosing this San Francisco travel guide. Inside, you'll uncover a treasure trove of sights to see, places to visit, and adventures to embark on at every turn. This comprehensive guide is packed with detailed addresses and phone numbers for the finest restaurants and accommodations, along

with clear directions to must-see attractions and hidden gems alike. Whether you're planning your next outing or seeking inspiration for your travels, this handy guide will be your trusted companion as you explore the beautiful and enchanting city of San Francisco. Get ready to make unforgettable memories and discover the magic that awaits in this extraordinary city!

San Francisco is a beautiful city that captivates visitors with its unique blend of charm, adventure, and history. Nestled along the stunning California coastline, this vibrant metropolis boasts an iconic skyline, rolling hills, and breathtaking views of the bay. Its rich cultural tapestry is woven with diverse neighborhoods, world-renowned landmarks, and a storied past that echoes through its streets.

Charm and Adventure
History, Geography, Weather, Culture, People
The rich history of San Francisco is evident in its well-preserved landmarks and historic sites. The infamous Alcatraz Island tells tales

of its past as a notorious federal prison, while Coit Tower stands as a monument to the city's resilience and artistic heritage. The Gold Rush era left an indelible mark on the city's development, and its legacy can still be felt in neighborhoods like the Barbary Coast and the Presidio. Walking through the streets, one can sense the layers of history that have shaped this remarkable city.

Points of Interest

San Francisco is home to countless points of interest that draw visitors from around the world. The majestic Golden Gate Bridge is a must-see, offering stunning views and photo opportunities. Alcatraz Island provides a fascinating glimpse into the past with its eerie prison cells and compelling stories. Union Square is the heart of the city's shopping and entertainment district, while the vibrant murals of the Mission District showcase the city's artistic soul. Fisherman's Wharf delights with its seafood restaurants, shops, and sea lions basking in the sun at Pier 39.

In addition to these well-known attractions, San Francisco offers hidden gems waiting to be discovered, such as the beautifully tiled Hidden Garden Steps, the tranquil Japanese Tea Garden, and the historic Sutro Baths ruins. Each corner of the city holds a new surprise, making every visit an unforgettable journey.

Early Days: Originally inhabited by the Ohlone people, San Francisco was claimed by the Spanish in 1776 when the Presidio and Mission San Francisco de Asís (Mission Dolores) were established.

Gold Rush: The 1849 Gold Rush transformed the city into a bustling metropolis almost overnight, bringing a diverse influx of settlers.

1906 Earthquake: A devastating earthquake and fire in 1906 destroyed much of the city, leading to significant rebuilding and growth.

Modern Era: The city became a hub for counterculture movements in the 1960s, including the Summer of Love, and later emerged as a center for technology and innovation.

Geography

Location: San Francisco is located on the northern end of the San Francisco Peninsula, surrounded by the Pacific Ocean to the west, San Francisco Bay to the east, and the Golden Gate to the north.

Landmarks: Known for its iconic landmarks such as the Golden Gate Bridge, Alcatraz Island, and steep hills adorned with cable cars.

Weather, important: San Francisco is renowned for its cool and often foggy weather influenced by its coastal location. The city experiences mild temperatures year-round, with summers typically cool and winters moderate. Due to rapid changes in microclimates across neighborhoods, it's essential to layer clothing when visiting. Even on a sunny day, temperatures can drop quickly, making it wise to carry a jacket or sweater to stay comfortable throughout the day.

Things to Pack and Bring with you when Touring San Francisco:

Layers of Clothing: San Francisco's weather can change rapidly throughout the day due to its microclimates. Bringing layers (like a light jacket, sweater, and scarf) ensures you're prepared for both sunny spells and chilly breezes.

Comfortable Walking Shoes: The city is known for its hilly terrain and many attractions are best explored on foot. Comfortable walking shoes or sneakers will keep you comfortable during your explorations.

Sun Protection: Even on cloudy days, UV rays can be strong. Pack sunscreen, sunglasses, and a hat to protect yourself from sunburn and glare while enjoying outdoor activities.

Reusable Water Bottle: Staying hydrated is crucial, especially if you're walking or biking around the city. Bring a reusable water bottle to refill at the city's many water stations and reduce plastic waste.

Map or Navigation App: San Francisco's layout can be confusing

with its hills and diverse neighborhoods. Bring a map or use a navigation app on your phone to easily find your way around and discover hidden gems.

Camera or Smartphone: The city offers countless photo opportunities—from the iconic Golden Gate Bridge to colorful Victorian houses. Capture memories with a camera or smartphone to cherish your trip.

Portable Charger: With so much to see and do, your phone's battery may drain quickly. Carry a portable charger to keep your devices powered up throughout the day.

Cash and Credit Cards: While most places in San Francisco accept credit cards, having some cash on hand is useful for small purchases, street vendors, and public transportation.

Guidebook or Travel App: Enhance your experience with a guidebook or travel app that provides insights into San Francisco's history, culture, and must-see attractions.

Snacks or Energy Bars: Exploring the city can work up an appetite. Pack snacks or energy bars to keep you fueled between meals and prevent hunger pangs.

Culture

Diversity: San Francisco is renowned for its cultural diversity, with significant Asian, Latinx, African American, and LGBTQ+ communities.

Arts: The city has a vibrant arts scene, including world-class museums like the San Francisco Museum of Modern Art (SFMOMA) and numerous galleries, theaters, and music venues.

Festivals: Hosts a variety of cultural festivals such as the Chinese New Year Parade, and Outside Lands Music Festival.

People

Population: Approximately 880,000 residents.

Demographics: A melting pot of ethnicities and cultures, with a significant percentage of foreign-born residents.

Innovation Hub: Home to many tech industry professionals and entrepreneurs, contributing to its reputation as a global innovation hub.

Culture:

Food Scene: Known for its diverse and innovative culinary scene, featuring everything from Michelin-starred restaurants to food trucks.

Music and Arts: Thriving live music scene and numerous art galleries and theaters.

Tech Influence: The presence of major tech companies and startups continues to shape the city's culture and economy.

People:

Friendly and Open-Minded: San Franciscans are known for their progressive attitudes and welcoming nature.

Community-Oriented: Strong sense of community with numerous neighborhood associations and local initiatives.

One could spend 2 Full Weeks Touring and Sightseeing San Francisco as it has that much to offer, so much Fun, and many Things to Do and See:

I hope this San Francisco travel guide fills you with excitement and a sense of adventure, offering countless places to explore, mouthwatering foods to savor, breathtaking hikes, serene beaches, and so many captivating sights to discover in San Francisco. May your journey be filled with unforgettable experiences and endless joy. Enjoy your visit!

The Golden Gate Bridge

Features: One of the most iconic landmarks in the world, the Golden Gate Bridge spans 1.7 miles across the Golden Gate Strait.

Experience: Walking or biking across the bridge offers stunning views of the bay, Alcatraz, and the city skyline. The bridge's art deco design and distinctive Orange color make it a visual delight.

Fun: Enjoy the exhilarating experience of walking or cycling across the bridge, visit the visitor centers on both ends, and take in the surrounding beauty from viewpoints like Battery Spencer and Fort Point.

Directions: From downtown, take Lombard Street/US-101 north toward the bridge. Follow signs for the Golden Gate Bridge visitor parking

2

Chapter 2. 15 Attractions to see and do at Pier 39 Fishermans Wharf

Pier 39 Address: Beach St &, Stockton St, San Francisco, CA 94133
Pier 39 Parking Garage: 2250 Powell St. San Francisco, CA. 94133

Sea Lions At Pier 39

Features: The docks at Pier 39 are home to a colony of California sea lions, which can be seen basking in the sun and playfully interacting with each other.

Experience: Watching the sea lions is a delight for visitors of all ages. The animals are often vocal and animated, creating a lively and engaging spectacle.

Fun: Enjoy observing their playful antics, take photos, and learn about their behavior through informational displays provided by the Pier 39 staff.

Pier 39

Features: Pier 39 features a variety of unique shops offering everything from San Francisco souvenirs to specialty foods, jewelry, clothing, and quirky gifts.

Experience: Strolling through the shops is a fun and eclectic experience. Each store has its own unique charm and offers an array of interesting products.

Fun: Find one-of-a-kind souvenirs, sample local treats, and enjoy the lively atmosphere as street performers entertain the crowds.

Pier 39 Restaurants

Features: The restaurants at Pier 39 offer a wide range of dining options, from casual eateries to fine dining, many with stunning views of San Francisco Bay and the Golden Gate Bridge.

Experience: Dining at Pier 39 provides not only delicious food but also beautiful waterfront views and a vibrant atmosphere. Seafood is a highlight, with many restaurants offering fresh, locally caught fish and shellfish.

Fun: Savor a meal with panoramic views, enjoy clam chowder in a sourdough bread bowl, and experience the lively energy of dining on the waterfront.

Aquarium of the Bay

Features: Located at Pier 39, this aquarium showcases the marine life of San Francisco Bay, including touch pools, walk-through tunnels, and interactive exhibits.

Experience: Visitors can get up close with a variety of sea creatures, from sharks and rays to jellyfish and sea otters. The walk-through tunnels provide an immersive underwater experience.

Fun: Touch sea stars and rays in the interactive touch pools, watch playful river otters, and be amazed by the diverse marine life in the walk-through tunnels.

Alcatraz Island Tour

Features: A historic island located in San Francisco Bay, Alcatraz is known for its infamous former prison, which once housed some of America's most notorious criminals.

Experience: The tour includes a ferry ride to the island, followed by a self-guided audio tour that narrates the history of the prison and stories of its inmates.

Fun: Explore the prison cells, learn about escape attempts, and take in stunning views of the city skyline and the Golden Gate Bridge from the island.

San Francisco Dungeon

Features: An interactive attraction that combines live actors, special effects, and rides to bring San Francisco's dark history to life.

Experience: The Dungeon provides a thrilling and immersive experience, guiding visitors through various historical events and legends with a mix of humor and horror.

Fun: Enjoy the thrill of the spooky storytelling, interactive exhibits, and the exhilarating drop ride that concludes the tour.

Musée Mécanique

Features: A unique museum featuring one of the world's largest collections of antique arcade games, mechanical musical instruments, and penny arcade machines.

Experience: Visitors can play hundreds of vintage games, from classic pinball machines to fortune tellers and mechanical dioramas.

Fun: Step back in time and enjoy the nostalgia of playing old-fashioned arcade games, listening to mechanical music, and exploring the quirky exhibits.

Ghirardelli Square

14

Features: A historic chocolate factory turned shopping and dining complex, offering stunning views of the bay and a variety of shops and restaurants.

Experience: Ghirardelli Square is a chocolate lover's paradise, with the Ghirardelli Chocolate Company offering delicious treats, sundaes, and hot chocolate.

Fun: Indulge in decadent chocolate desserts, explore the boutique shops, and enjoy the beautiful bay views from the outdoor seating areas.

Madame Tussauds Wax Museum

Features: A museum featuring lifelike wax figures of celebrities, historical figures, and cultural icons.

Experience: The wax figures are incredibly realistic, allowing visitors to get up close and personal with their favorite stars for photos.

Fun: Pose with lifelike figures of your favorite celebrities, experience themed exhibits, and learn about the art of wax sculpting.

Ripley's Believe It or Not!

Features: A museum showcasing oddities and bizarre artifacts from around the world, with interactive exhibits and hands-on activities.

Experience: Ripley's offers a fascinating and fun experience, filled with strange and unusual displays that challenge the imagination.

Fun: Explore the quirky exhibits, participate in interactive displays, and be amazed by the odd and unusual items on display.

Cable Car Ride

Hop on a cable car located at the turntable at the end of Hyde Street (near Ghirardelli Square)

Features: San Francisco's iconic cable cars offer a unique way to explore the city, with routes that provide stunning views of the city's hills and waterfront.

Experience: Riding a cable car is both nostalgic and exciting, offering a moving glimpse into the city's past while navigating its steep streets.

Fun: Enjoy the thrill of riding up and down San Francisco's steep hills, hang off the side of the car for an authentic experience, and take in the scenic views along the way.

Bike Rentals and Tours

Bay City Bike Rentals and Tours
Address: 2661 Taylor Street, San Francisco, CA 94133
Phone: (415) 346-2453

Bay City Bike Rentals and Tours
Address: 501 Bay Street, San Francisco, CA 94133
Phone: (415) 346-2453

Blazing Saddles Bike Rentals and Tours
Address: 2715 Hyde Street, San Francisco, CA 94109
Phone: (415) 202-8888

Features: Numerous rental shops around San Francisco offer bikes for exploring the city, with options for guided tours and self-guided adventures.

Experience: Renting a bike allows visitors to experience the city's scenic beauty at their own pace. Popular routes include the waterfront along the Embarcadero, through Golden Gate Park, and across the

18

Golden Gate Bridge to Sausalito.

Fun: Biking provides an active and adventurous way to see the city's sights. Enjoy the fresh air, stop at scenic viewpoints, and explore hidden gems that are easily accessible by bike.

Bay Cruises

Features: Bay cruises depart from several locations, including Fisherman's Wharf and Pier 39, offering different types of cruises such as sightseeing, sunset, and dinner cruises.

Experience: A Bay cruise offers stunning views of San Francisco's iconic landmarks, including the Golden Gate Bridge, Alcatraz Island, and the city skyline. The cruises are often narrated, providing historical and cultural insights.

Fun: Relax on the deck with the wind in your hair, capture breathtaking photos, and enjoy a different perspective of the city from the water. Some cruises offer dining and live music, enhancing the experience.

Street Performers

Features: San Francisco's street performers can be found in popular areas such as Pier 39, Fisherman's Wharf, and Union Square, showcasing a variety of talents including music, magic, juggling, and more.

Experience: Watching street performers adds a lively and dynamic element to the city's atmosphere. Performers often engage with the audience, making each show interactive and unique.

Fun: Enjoy the spontaneous entertainment as you explore the city. Street performances are family-friendly and offer a chance to see diverse talents and creativity in action.

3

Chapter 3. Haight Ashbury and Golden Gate Park

Haight-Ashbury is located right at the beginning entrance to Golden Gate Park

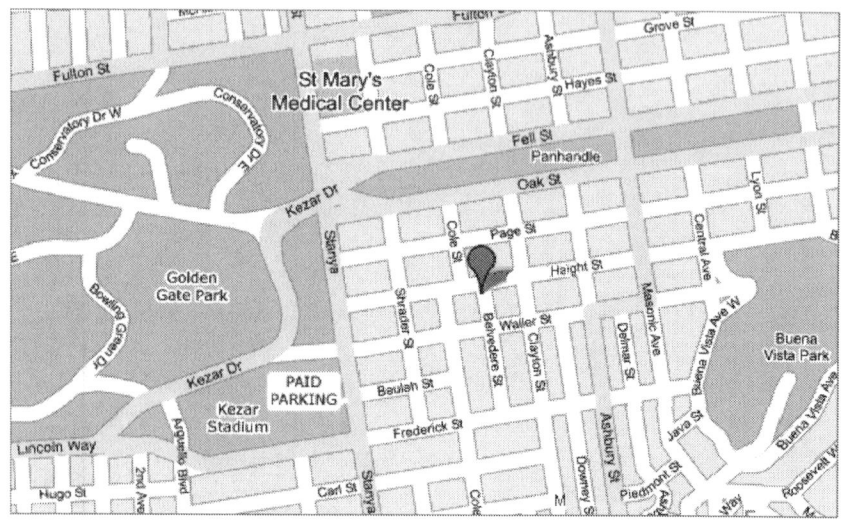

Haight Ashbury

Features: Known as the epicenter of the 1960s counterculture movement, Haight-Ashbury is rich with history, eclectic shops, vintage clothing stores, colorful murals, and historic Victorian houses.

Experience: Walking through Haight-Ashbury feels like stepping back in time. You'll find an array of unique boutiques, record stores, and vibrant street art. The atmosphere is laid-back and bohemian, often filled with live music and street performers.

Fun: Explore the legendary music scene that once hosted bands like The Grateful Dead and Jefferson Airplane. Discover quirky shops and enjoy people-watching in this lively neighborhood.

Conservatory of Flowers

Features: Located in Golden Gate Park, the Conservatory of Flowers is a stunning Victorian greenhouse housing an extensive collection of rare and exotic plants.

Experience: Strolling through the conservatory, you'll encounter lush tropical plants, vibrant flowers, and unique flora from around the world. The atmosphere is tranquil and educational.

Fun: Marvel at the beauty of the meticulously maintained gardens, participate in guided tours, and enjoy seasonal exhibits that highlight different plant species.

de Young Museum

Features: A fine arts museum located in Golden Gate Park, the de Young Museum features American art from the 17th through the 21st centuries, contemporary art, and international textiles.

Experience: The museum offers a rich cultural experience with its diverse collection of artworks. The architecture of the museum itself is impressive, with a striking copper facade and an observation tower providing panoramic views of the city.

Fun: Engage with interactive exhibits, attend art workshops and lectures, and enjoy the breathtaking views from the Hamon Observation Tower.

Japanese Tea Garden

Features: This serene garden in Golden Gate Park features traditional Japanese landscaping, koi ponds, pagodas, stone lanterns, and a teahouse.

Experience: The Japanese Tea Garden offers a peaceful retreat with its beautifully manicured gardens and tranquil atmosphere. The authentic design and layout provide a cultural immersion.

Fun: Walk across the arched drum bridge, enjoy a cup of tea in the teahouse, and take in the beauty of the cherry blossoms and other seasonal flora.

Koret Children's Quarter and Carousel

Features: This playground in Golden Gate Park includes a historic carousel, climbing structures, slides, and swings designed for children.

Experience: The Koret Children's Quarter is a haven for families, offering a safe and fun environment for kids to play and explore. The charming carousel adds a nostalgic touch.

Fun: Watch children enjoy the various play structures, ride the whimsical carousel, and picnic in the surrounding grassy areas.

San Francisco Botanical Garden

Features: Spanning 55 acres in Golden Gate Park, the San Francisco Botanical Garden features over 8,000 different plant species from around the world.

Experience: Walking through the botanical garden, visitors can explore diverse plant collections, including Mediterranean, cloud forest, and temperate climate gardens. The garden is peaceful and educational.

Fun: Participate in guided tours, attend gardening workshops, and enjoy seasonal plant sales and events.

Musical Concourse

Features: Located between the de Young Museum and the California Academy of Sciences in Golden Gate Park, the Music Concourse is an open-air plaza with fountains, statues, and a historic bandshell.

Experience: The Music Concourse serves as a cultural hub with its elegant design and ample space for public gatherings. It's a great spot to relax and enjoy the surroundings.

Fun: Attend free concerts and performances in the bandshell, explore the fountains and sculptures, and relax on the benches under the shade of the trees.

California Academy of Sciences

Features: A natural history museum, aquarium, planetarium, and research institution all under one living roof in Golden Gate Park.

Experience: The California Academy of Sciences offers a comprehensive and interactive educational experience. Visitors can explore the aquarium with its vibrant marine life, the planetarium for stunning space shows, and the natural history exhibits.

Fun: Engage with hands-on exhibits, watch a show in the planetarium, marvel at the Steinhart Aquarium's diverse marine life, and walk through the four-story Osher Rainforest.

Osher Rain Forest at The California Academy of Sciences

Features: A four-story living rainforest exhibit inside the California Academy of Sciences, featuring tropical plants, free-flying birds, and butterflies.

Experience: Stepping into the Osher Rainforest is like entering a lush, tropical environment. The humidity, sounds, and sights of the rainforest are immersive and educational.

Fun: Walk through the spiraling pathway from the forest floor to the canopy, observe the exotic animals and plants, and enjoy the butterfly house where butterflies flutter around freely.

4

Chapter 4. Attractions by The Cliff House, Ocean Beach, Sutro Baths, Sutro Heights, Lands End Trail and Eagles Point, all located near The Cliff House.

The Cliff House

Features: A historic restaurant perched on a cliff overlooking the Pacific Ocean, offering stunning views and a rich history dating back to 1863.

Experience: Dining at The Cliff House provides breathtaking ocean views, especially during sunset, along with a menu featuring seafood and California cuisine.

Fun: Enjoy a meal with panoramic ocean views, explore the history of the building, and take a walk along the nearby coastal trails.

Ocean Beach

Features: A 3.5-mile stretch of beach along the western edge of San Francisco, known for its scenic beauty and strong surf.

Experience: Ocean Beach offers a tranquil escape with its wide sandy shore, often enveloped in mist and frequented by surfers and beachcombers.

Fun: Walk along the beach, watch surfers ride the waves, have a bonfire in designated areas, and enjoy the natural beauty of the Pacific Ocean.

Sutro Baths

Features: The ruins of a large, historic public bathhouse complex built in the 1890s, located near the Cliff House.

Experience: Exploring the Sutro Baths provides a glimpse into San Francisco's past, with ruins set against a dramatic coastal backdrop

Fun: Wander through the ruins, take photos of the stunning scenery, and hike the surrounding trails for panoramic views of the coastline.

Sutro Heights

Features: A historic park located above the Sutro Baths, featuring landscaped gardens, statues, and remnants of Adolph Sutro's mansion.

Experience: Sutro Heights offers a peaceful and scenic spot with lush gardens, historical artifacts, and stunning ocean views.

Fun: Stroll through the gardens, enjoy a picnic with a birds eye view, high above the beach and explore the historical landmarks within the park.

Address: Sutro Heights Park, 48th Ave & Point Lobos Ave, San Francisco, CA 94121, USA

Directions: Sutro Heights Park is located in the Outer Richmond District of San Francisco. From downtown San Francisco, take Geary Boulevard westbound and continue onto Point Lobos Avenue. Sutro Heights Park will be on your right. (right near The Cliff House)

Camera Obscura and Holographic Gallery

Features: A historic optical device located near the Cliff House that provides a 360-degree view of the surrounding area, and a gallery showcasing holograms.

Experience: The Camera Obscura offers a unique and fascinating way to see the coastline, using mirrors and lenses to project live images onto a viewing table.

Fun: View the live panorama inside the Camera Obscura, explore the holographic gallery, and learn about the history and science behind these optical marvels.

Located at The Cliff House.

Lands End Trail and Eagles Point

Features: A scenic trail along the rugged coastline of San Francisco, offering stunning views of the Golden Gate Bridge, hidden beaches, and historical landmarks.

Experience: Hiking the Lands End Trail provides breathtaking vistas, diverse plant life, and opportunities to explore historical shipwrecks and the USS San Francisco Memorial.

Fun: Enjoy a hike with spectacular views, visit Eagles Point for a panoramic lookout, and discover hidden gems like Mile Rock Beach and the labyrinth at Lands End.

Address: Eagles Point, El Camino Del Mar & 32nd Ave, San Francisco, CA 94121, USA

Directions: Eagle's Point is part of the Lands End trail in the Outer Richmond District of San Francisco. From downtown San Francisco, take Geary Boulevard westbound, turn left onto 32nd Avenue, and continue to El Camino Del Mar. Park along El Camino Del Mar and follow signs to the trailhead for Lands End and Eagle's Point.

5

Chapter 5. Hidden Gems

Twin Peaks

Features: Twin Peaks consists of two prominent hills offering panoramic views of San Francisco and beyond.

Experience: A visit to Twin Peaks provides breathtaking 360-degree views of the city, including downtown San Francisco, the Golden Gate Bridge, Alcatraz, and the Bay Bridge. The vantage point is particularly stunning at sunrise and sunset.

Fun: Drive or hike to the top, take in the expansive views, and capture beautiful photos. On clear days, the visibility is exceptional, making it a perfect spot for sightseeing.

Address: Twin Peaks Blvd, San Francisco, CA 94114

Directions: From downtown, take Market Street south to Castro Street, turn right onto 17th Street, then left onto Clayton Street, and continue up Twin Peaks Blvd.

Lombard Street

Features: Known as the "crookedest street in the world," Lombard Street features eight sharp hairpin turns in a steep, one-block section.

Experience: Driving down Lombard Street is a thrilling experience due to its tight turns and steep incline. The beautifully landscaped gardens along the curves add to the charm.

Fun: Walk down the sidewalks for a closer look at the stunning gardens, watch cars navigate the twists and turns, and take photos from the bottom of the street looking up.

Address: Lombard St, between Hyde St and Leavenworth St, San Francisco, CA 94133

Directions: From downtown, take Hyde Street north to Lombard Street. The crooked section is between Hyde and Leavenworth Streets.

Coit Tower

Features: A white, fluted column tower located atop Telegraph Hill, offering an observation deck with panoramic views of the city.

Experience: Inside the tower, visitors can admire murals painted in the 1930s depicting life in California during the Great Depression. The observation deck provides sweeping views of San Francisco.

Fun: Take the elevator to the top for the best views, explore the historical murals, and enjoy the scenic Filbert Steps leading up to the tower through lush gardens.

Address: 1 Telegraph Hill Blvd, San Francisco, CA 94133

Directions: From downtown, take Columbus Avenue north, turn left onto Filbert Street, and follow the signs to Coit Tower.

Chinatown

Features: San Francisco's Chinatown is the oldest and one of the largest in North America, featuring vibrant streets, shops, temples, and restaurants.

Experience: Walking through Chinatown feels like stepping into another world with its bustling markets, traditional architecture, and cultural landmarks.

Fun: Visit the Golden Gate Fortune Cookie Factory, explore herbal shops and tea houses, dine at authentic Chinese restaurants, and enjoy the colorful festivals and parades.

Address: Grant Ave and Bush St, San Francisco, CA 94108

Directions: From downtown, walk or drive north on Grant Avenue, the main thoroughfare through Chinatown.

Union Square

Features: A bustling plaza surrounded by upscale shops, hotels, theaters, and restaurants in downtown San Francisco.

Experience: Union Square is a shopper's paradise, featuring luxury brands, department stores, and unique boutiques. The square itself hosts public events and seasonal ice skating.

Fun: Shop till you drop, attend live events and performances, dine at a variety of restaurants, and enjoy the vibrant urban atmosphere.

Address: 333 Post St, San Francisco, CA 94108

Directions: Located in downtown, bounded by Geary, Powell, Post, and Stockton Streets. Easily accessible by public transit, including BART and Muni.

Hidden Garden Steps

Features: A beautiful mosaic staircase located in the Inner Sunset district, decorated with colorful tiles depicting flowers, animals, and other natural elements.

Experience: Climbing the Hidden Garden Steps is both a workout and an art appreciation activity. Each step is intricately decorated, creating a stunning visual effect.

Fun: Admire the detailed mosaics, take photos of the vibrant artwork, and enjoy the sense of discovery as you climb.

Address: 16th Ave and Kirkham St, San Francisco, CA 94122

Directions: From downtown, take Judah Street west, turn right on 16th Avenue, and the steps are between Kirkham and Lawton Streets.

The Painted Ladies

Features: A row of Victorian houses famously known as the "Painted Ladies," located on Steiner Street across from Alamo Square Park.

Experience: These beautifully restored and brightly colored houses are an iconic symbol of San Francisco's architectural heritage.

Fun: Relax in Alamo Square Park with a perfect view of the Painted Ladies and the city skyline in the background, and snap photos of these picturesque homes.

Address: Steiner St and Hayes St, San Francisco, CA 94117

Directions: From downtown, take Fulton Street west, turn left on Steiner Street, and the Painted Ladies are located along the east side of Alamo Square Park.

Muir Woods

Features: A national monument located just north of San Francisco, home to ancient coast redwood trees.

Experience: Walking through Muir Woods is a serene and awe-inspiring experience, with towering redwoods and a tranquil atmosphere.

Fun: Hike the well-maintained trails, marvel at the giant trees, and enjoy the peaceful natural environment. It's a great spot for nature photography and bird watching.

Address: 1 Muir Woods Rd, Mill Valley, CA 94941

Directions: From San Francisco, take US-101 north, exit at CA-1/Stinson Beach, follow signs to Muir Woods.

Point Bonita

Features: A historic lighthouse located at the entrance to San Francisco Bay, part of the Golden Gate National Recreation Area.

Experience: The walk to Point Bonita Lighthouse includes a dramatic suspension bridge and stunning coastal views.

Fun: Explore the lighthouse, learn about its history, and enjoy the breathtaking ocean and bay views along the way.

Address: Point Bonita Lighthouse, Sausalito, CA 94965

Directions: From San Francisco, take US-101 north to the Marin Headlands exit, follow signs to Point Bonita Lighthouse.

Marin Headlands

Features: A hilly peninsula located north of the Golden Gate Bridge, offering stunning views, hiking trails, and historic military sites.

Experience: The Marin Headlands provide some of the best vantage points for views of the Golden Gate Bridge, the Pacific Ocean, and San Francisco.

Fun: Hike the scenic trails, visit historical sites like Battery Spencer and the Nike Missile Site, and watch for wildlife such as deer and hawks.

Address: Marin Headlands, Sausalito, CA 94965 **Directions**: From San Francisco, take US-101 north, exit at Alexander Avenue, follow signs to Marin Headlands.

6

Chapter 6. Top Hikes and Walking Tours, Inspiring and Beautiful

Lands End Trail

Features: A scenic coastal trail with breathtaking views of the Golden Gate Bridge, hidden beaches, and the ruins of the Sutro Baths.

Experience: This trail offers a mix of forested areas and dramatic ocean views, with plenty of spots to rest and take in the scenery.

Fun: Hike the winding paths, visit the Lands End Labyrinth, explore the Sutro Baths ruins, and enjoy panoramic vistas of the Pacific Ocean and Golden Gate Bridge.

Address: 680 Point Lobos Ave, San Francisco, CA 94121

Directions: From downtown, take Geary Blvd west to 32nd Ave, turn right, and then left onto Point Lobos Ave. The trailhead is at the Lands End Lookout Visitor Center.

Golden Gate Park

Features: A large urban park with gardens, lakes, museums, and cultural attractions spread over 1,017 acres.

Experience: Walking through Golden Gate Park provides a diverse range of experiences, from the peaceful Japanese Tea Garden to the bustling Music Concourse.

Fun: Explore the Conservatory of Flowers, visit the de Young Museum, relax at Stow Lake, and discover hidden gems like the Shakespeare Garden and Strawberry Hill.

Address: 501 Stanyan St, San Francisco, CA 94117

Directions: From downtown, take Fell St west to Stanyan St, which marks the eastern entrance to the park.

Presidio of San Francisco

Features: A historic park and former military base offering scenic trails, historic buildings, and stunning views of the Golden Gate Bridge.

Experience: The Presidio's extensive trail network takes you through forests, coastal bluffs, and historic sites, with plenty of interpretive signs along the way.

Fun: Walk the Presidio's main trails like the Ecology Trail, Lovers' Lane, and the Bay Area Ridge Trail. Don't miss the views from the Golden Gate Overlook and the Presidio Promenade.

Address: 103 Montgomery St, San Francisco, CA 94129

Directions: From downtown, take Lombard St west, turn right onto Lyon St, and follow signs for the Presidio.

Glen Canyon Park

Features: A natural canyon with rugged trails, lush vegetation, and a creek running through it.

Experience: This hidden gem offers a wilderness escape within the city, with trails that wind through a diverse landscape of rock formations, meadows, and forests.

Fun: Hike the Islais Creek Trail, explore the rocky outcrops, and enjoy the natural beauty of the canyon. Great for spotting wildlife and enjoying a quiet retreat.

Address: Elk St & Chenery St, San Francisco, CA 94127

Directions: From downtown, take Market St southwest to Portola Dr, turn left onto Glen Canyon Rd, and then right onto Elk St.

Mount Sutro Open Space Reserve

Features: A forested area with trails winding through dense eucalyptus groves and offering city views.

Experience: The trails in Mount Sutro Open Space Reserve provide a peaceful escape with a network of paths that are perfect for hiking and trail running.

Fun: Explore the historic Sutro Forest, enjoy the cool, shaded trails, and take in views of the city from the higher points. The area is also known for its rich birdlife and plant diversity.

Address: 476 Johnstone Dr, San Francisco, CA 94131

Directions: From downtown, take Market St southwest to 17th St, then continue on Stanyan St to Johnstone Dr.

Crissy Field

Features: A former airfield turned into a popular waterfront park with beaches, picnic areas, and walking paths.

Experience: Walking along Crissy Field offers stunning views of the Golden Gate Bridge, Alcatraz, and the San Francisco skyline. The flat, accessible paths are ideal for leisurely strolls.

Fun: Walk or bike along the Golden Gate Promenade, relax on the beach, have a picnic, and watch windsurfers and kiteboarders in the bay.

Address: 1199 E Beach, San Francisco, CA 94129

Directions: From downtown, take Lombard St west, turn right onto Lyon St, and follow signs for Crissy Field.

Marin Headlands

Features: A hilly peninsula offering dramatic coastal views, historic military sites, and diverse wildlife.

Experience: The Marin Headlands provide some of the best vantage points for views of the Golden Gate Bridge, the Pacific Ocean, and San Francisco.

Fun: Hike the scenic trails, visit historical sites like Battery Spencer and the Nike Missile Site, and watch for wildlife such as deer and hawks. The area is also great for photography and picnicking.

Address: Conzelman Rd, Sausalito, CA 94965

Directions: From San Francisco, take US-101 north to the Marin Headlands exit, follow signs for Conzelman Rd.

Bernal Heights Park

Features: A hilltop park offering panoramic views of San Francisco and the bay.

Experience: Hiking to the top of Bernal Heights Park provides stunning views and a sense of accomplishment. The park's open space and grassy areas are perfect for picnics and relaxation.

Fun: Enjoy a moderate hike to the summit, take in the 360-degree views, and relax on the grassy slopes. The park is also popular with dog walkers and families.

Address: 3400-3416 Folsom St, San Francisco, CA 94110 **Directions**: From downtown, take Mission St south, turn left onto Cesar Chavez St, and then right onto Folsom St to reach the park entrance.

Filbert Steps

Features: A steep staircase that climbs Telegraph Hill, lined with lush gardens and offering views of the bay.

Experience: Climbing the Filbert Steps is both a workout and a scenic journey, with beautifully maintained gardens and historic homes along the way.

Fun: Ascend the steps, explore the gardens, and enjoy the views from Coit Tower at the top. The steps are also a great place to spot parrots and other birds.

Address: Filbert St & Sansome St, San Francisco, CA 94133

Directions: From downtown, take Battery St north, turn left onto Filbert St, and the steps begin at the intersection with Sansome St.

Lover's Lane

Features: A historic trail in the Presidio, lined with eucalyptus trees and offering a peaceful, scenic walk.

Experience: Lover's Lane is a short but picturesque trail that provides a tranquil escape, with beautiful surroundings and a sense of history.

Fun: Walk the scenic path, enjoy the tranquility, and discover the nearby Andy Goldsworthy's Wood Line art installation.

Address: 3753 Army Rd, San Francisco, CA 94129

Directions: From downtown, take Lombard St west, turn right onto Presidio Blvd, and then right onto Army Rd to find Lover's Lane.

7

Chapter 7. The Best Beaches

Baker Beach
  Address: 1774 Gibson Rd, San Francisco, CA 94129

Features and Experience:

Scenic Views: Offers stunning views of the Golden Gate Bridge, the Marin Headlands, and the Pacific Ocean.

Picnicking: Picnic areas with barbecue pits are available, making it perfect for a beach day with family and friends.

Wildlife: You might spot dolphins, sea lions, and various seabirds.

Nudity: The northern end of Baker Beach is clothing-optional.

Fun Activities:

Photography: The views of the Golden Gate Bridge are perfect for photographers.

Fishing: The beach is a popular spot for surf fishing.

Hiking: There are nearby trails that offer great hikes and scenic overlooks.

Directions:

By Car: From downtown San Francisco, take US-101 North and exit at Merchant Road. Continue on Lincoln Blvd, then take a left onto Bowley St and follow signs to Baker Beach.

Public Transport: Take the 38-Geary bus to 25th Ave & California St, then walk through Lincoln Park to reach the beach.

Ocean Beach

Address: Great Hwy, San Francisco, CA 94121

Features and Experience:

Length: This is a long, sandy beach stretching 3.5 miles along the western edge of San Francisco.

Surfing: Popular among surfers due to its strong waves.

Bonfires: Bonfire rings are available for use, allowing for cozy beach bonfires.

Fun Activities:

Surfing: Ideal for experienced surfers.

Kite Flying: The windy conditions make it great for kite flying.

Walking and Jogging: The long stretch of beach is perfect for walks or runs.

Directions:

By Car: From downtown, take Fulton St west until you hit the Great Highway, which runs along Ocean Beach.

Public Transport: Take the N-Judah Muni line to Judah St & La Playa St, or the 5-Fulton bus to La Playa & Cabrillo St.

China Beach

Address: 490 Sea Cliff Ave, San Francisco, CA 94121

Features and Experience:

Secluded: Smaller and more secluded than other beaches, offering a quieter experience.

Golden Gate Views: Offers views of the Golden Gate Bridge, particularly beautiful at sunset.

Facilities: Picnic areas, restrooms, and showers are available.

Fun Activities:

Swimming: The waters here are calmer, making it safer for swimming.

Picnicking: The picnic area is a great spot for a quiet lunch.

Photography: Beautiful views make it a great spot for photography.

Directions:

By Car: From downtown, take US-101 North, exit at 25th Ave, then continue on Lincoln Blvd to Sea Cliff Ave.

Public Transport: Take the 1-California bus to 30th Ave & California

St, then walk down to China Beach.

Crissy Field Beach

Address: 1199 E Beach, San Francisco, CA 94129

Features and Experience:

Golden Gate Views: Offers unparalleled views of the Golden Gate Bridge.

Accessibility: Easily accessible with paved paths suitable for walking, biking, and wheelchair access.

Wildlife: Often frequented by birds and occasionally marine mammals.

Fun Activities:

Walking and Biking: Paved paths make it ideal for walking and biking.

Picnicking: Picnic tables and a large grassy area make it great for picnics.

Water Sports: Popular for kayaking and paddleboarding.

Directions:

By Car: From downtown, take Marina Blvd to Mason St, then follow signs to Crissy Field.

Public Transport: Take the 30-Stockton bus to Broderick St & Beach St, then walk to the beach.

Marshall's Beach

Address: Langdon Ct, San Francisco, CA 94129

Features and Experience:

Seclusion: One of the more secluded beaches in San Francisco, providing a tranquil environment.

Golden Gate Views: Offers some of the best views of the Golden Gate Bridge.

Nudity: Known for being a clothing-optional beach.

Fun Activities:

Photography: Stunning views of the Golden Gate Bridge are perfect for photos.

Hiking: Accessible via the Batteries to Bluffs Trail, making it a great hiking destination.

Relaxation: Its seclusion makes it ideal for a quiet day of relaxation.

Directions:

By Car: From downtown, take US-101 North and exit at Merchant Rd, then follow Lincoln Blvd to Langdon Ct.

Public Transport: Take the 28-19th Avenue bus to the Golden Gate Bridge Toll Plaza, then walk to the beach.

8

Chapter 8. San Francisco at Night

San Francisco is a vibrant city with a plethora of activities to enjoy at night. Here are some of the top things to do and see in San Francisco after the sun sets:

Golden Gate Bridge at Night

Address: Golden Gate Bridge, San Francisco, CA 94129 **Telephone:** (415) 921-5858

Features and Experience:

Illumination: The bridge is beautifully illuminated at night, providing a stunning view.

Walking and Biking: Enjoy a nighttime walk or bike ride across the bridge.

Photography: Great for night photography with views of the city skyline.

Fun Activities:

Night Walks: Experience the tranquility and beauty of the bridge at night.

Scenic Views: Enjoy panoramic views of the San Francisco Bay and city lights.

Exploratorium After Dark

Address: Pier 15, The Embarcadero, San Francisco, CA 94111
Telephone: (415) 528-4444

Features and Experience:

Adult-Only Event: Every Thursday night, the Exploratorium hosts an adults-only event with themed exhibits and activities.

Interactive Exhibits: Engage with hands-on science and art exhibits.

Live Music and Performances: Enjoy live music, performances, and special events.

Fun Activities:

Interactive Learning: Explore exhibits and learn through interactive experiences.

Socializing: A great place to meet new people and socialize in a unique setting.

Twin Peaks

Address: 501 Twin Peaks Blvd, San Francisco, CA 94114 **Telephone:** (415) 831-2700

Features and Experience:

Panoramic Views: Offers breathtaking 360-degree views of San Francisco.

Nighttime Vistas: See the city lights and landmarks illuminated at night.

Stargazing: A great spot for stargazing on clear nights.

Fun Activities:

Night Photography: Capture stunning photos of the city skyline.

Romantic Outing: Ideal for a romantic evening with a view.

Chinatown Night Market

Address: Grant Ave and Broadway, San Francisco, CA 94108
Telephone: (415) 982-6306

Features and Experience:

Cultural Experience: Immerse yourself in the vibrant culture of Chinatown.

Street Food: Enjoy a variety of street food vendors offering delicious eats.

Shopping: Browse through stalls selling unique goods and souvenirs.

Fun Activities:

Culinary Adventure: Try different types of Chinese street food and delicacies.

Shopping: Find unique gifts and souvenirs to take home.

San Francisco Symphony

Address: 201 Van Ness Ave, San Francisco, CA 94102 **Telephone:** (415) 864-6000

Features and Experience:

World-Class Performances: Enjoy performances by one of the leading symphonies in the world.

Historic Venue: Experience the beautiful and historic Davies Symphony Hall.

variety of Music: Programs range from classical symphonies to contemporary works.

Fun Activities:

Concerts: Enjoy an evening of beautiful music and culture.

Special Events: Attend special themed nights and events throughout the year.

Alcatraz Night Tour

Address: Pier 33, Alcatraz Landing, San Francisco, CA 94111
Telephone: (415) 981-7625

Features and Experience:

Historic Tour: Explore the infamous Alcatraz Island and prison with a guided night tour.

Unique Atmosphere: Experience the island in the eerie ambiance of the night. .

Fun Activities:

History and Mystery: Learn about the history and legends of Alcatraz.

Scenic Views: Enjoy views of the city skyline and Bay Bridge illuminated at night.

Club Fugazi - "Dear San Francisco" Show

Address: 678 Green St, San Francisco, CA 94133 **Telephone:** (415) 273-0600

Features and Experience:

Theatrical Performance: A high-energy acrobatic show celebrating the spirit of San Francisco.

Intimate Venue: The historic Club Fugazi offers an intimate setting for the performance.

Audience Interaction: Engaging and interactive with the audience.

Fun Activities:

Live Entertainment: Enjoy a unique and entertaining live performance.

Cultural Experience: Gain a deeper appreciation for the culture and history of San Francisco.

North Beach Nightlife

Address: Columbus Ave, San Francisco, CA 94133 **Telephone:** Varies by venue

Features and Experience:

Lively Neighborhood: Known for its vibrant nightlife and Italian heritage.

Bars and Clubs: A variety of bars, clubs, and live music venues.

Dining: Numerous restaurants offering Italian cuisine and more.

Fun Activities:

Bar Hopping: Explore different bars and clubs in the area.

Live Music: Enjoy live music performances in various venues.

Dining: Savor delicious meals at renowned restaurants.

AT&T Park Night Game

Address: 24 Willie Mays Plaza, San Francisco, CA 94107 **Telephone:** (415) 972-2000

Features and Experience:

Major League Baseball: Home to the San Francisco Giants, offering an exciting game day atmosphere.

Stadium Views: Spectacular views of the Bay from the stadium.

Entertainment: Pre-game and in-game entertainment for all ages.

Fun Activities:

Baseball Game: Enjoy a thrilling night game with the Giants.

Stadium Experience: Explore the stadium, food vendors, and fan activities.

Night-time Cable Cars

Address: Powell and Market St, San Francisco, CA 94102 **Telephone:** (415) 701-2311

Features and Experience:

Historic Ride: Experience a ride on San Francisco's historic cable cars.

City Views: Enjoy nighttime views of the city's streets and landmarks.

Unique Experience: A quintessential San Francisco experience.

Fun Activities:

Sightseeing: See the city's sights illuminated at night.

Historic Ride: Learn about the history and operation of the cable cars.

9

Chapter 9. Top 30 Best Restaurants in San Francisco

1. **Zuni Café**

Cuisine: Californian

Why it's good: Famous for its roast chicken and Caesar salad, offering a seasonal menu with locally sourced ingredients.

Address: 1658 Market St, San Francisco, CA 94102

Phone: (415) 552-2522

2. Tadich Grill

Cuisine: Seafood

Why it's good: One of the oldest restaurants in San Francisco, known for its cioppino and seafood-centric dishes.

Address: 240 California St, San Francisco, CA 94111

Phone: (415) 391-1849

3. Gary Danko

Cuisine: Contemporary American

Why it's good: Michelin-starred fine dining with impeccable service and an exquisite tasting menu.

Address: 800 North Point St, San Francisco, CA 94109

Phone: (415) 749-2060

4. State Bird Provision's

Cuisine: Californian

Why it's good: Innovative dim sum-style service with creative, flavorful small plates.

Address: 1529 Fillmore St, San Francisco, CA 94115 **Phone**: (415) 795-1272

5. Swan Oyster Depot

Cuisine: Seafood

Why it's good: Legendary seafood counter known for its fresh oysters, clam chowder, and crab.

Address:1517 Polk St, San Francisco, CA 94109 **Phone**: (415) 673-1101

6. Kokkari Estiatorio

Cuisine: Greek

Why it's good: Rustic yet elegant dining experience with authentic Greek dishes and a warm atmosphere.

Address: 200 Jackson St, San Francisco, CA 94111 **Phone**: (415) 981-0983

7. Nopa

Cuisine: Californian

Why it's good: Popular late-night spot with a wood-fired oven and a menu featuring locally sourced ingredients.

Address: 560 Divisadero St, San Francisco, CA 94117

Phone: (415) 864-8643

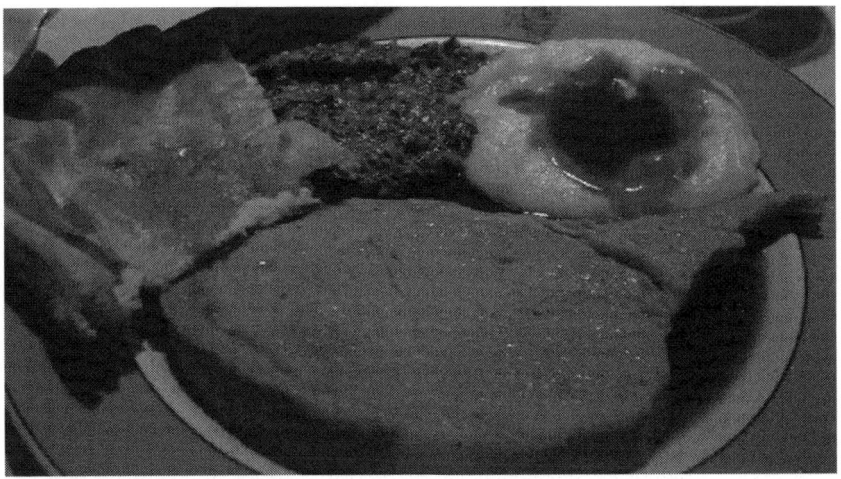

8. House of Prime Rib

Cuisine: Steakhouse

Why it's good: Classic steakhouse renowned for its prime rib and traditional English-style service.

Address: 1906 Van Ness Ave, San Francisco, CA 94109 **Phone**: (415) 885-4605

9. La Taqueria

Cuisine: Mexican

Why it's good: Famous for its Mission-style burritos and tacos, often considered some of the best in the city.

Address: 2889 Mission St, San Francisco, CA 94110

Phone: (415) 285-7117

10. Foreign Cinema

Cuisine: Californian

Why it's good: Unique dining experience with outdoor movie screenings and a menu featuring seasonal ingredients.

Address: 2534 Mission St, San Francisco, CA 94110

Phone: (415) 648-7600

11. Boulevard

Cuisine: American

Why it's good: Elegant restaurant with a focus on contemporary American cuisine and beautiful views of the Bay Bridge.

Address: 1 Mission St, San Francisco, CA 94105 **Phone**: (415) 543-6084

12.Tartine Bakery Bakery/Café

Why it's good: World-renowned bakery known for its artisanal bread, pastries, and coffee.

Address: 600 Guerrero St, San Francisco, CA 94110 **Phone**: (415)

487-2600

13. Rich Table

Cuisine: Californian

Why it's good: Creative dishes made with locally sourced ingredients, offering a relaxed yet refined dining experience.

Address: 199 Gough St, San Francisco, CA 94102 **Phone**: (415) 355-9085

14. Liholiho Yacht Club

Cuisine: Hawaiian/Asian Fusion

Why it's good: Vibrant atmosphere with a menu blending Hawaiian, Indian, and Californian influences.

Address: 871 Sutter St, San Francisco, CA 94109

Phone: (415) 440-5446

15. Saison

Cuisine: Contemporary American

Why it's good: Michelin-starred restaurant with a focus on fire cooking and an ever-evolving tasting menu.

Address: 178 Townsend St, San Francisco, CA 94107 **Phone**: (415) 828-7990

16. Benu

Cuisine: Contemporary Asian

Why it's good: Three-Michelin-starred restaurant offering an innovative tasting menu with Asian influences.

Address: 22 Hawthorne St, San Francisco, CA 94105

Phone: (415) 685-4860

17. The Slanted Door

Cuisine: Vietnamese

Why it's good: Modern Vietnamese cuisine with a focus on fresh, high-quality ingredients and waterfront views.

Address: 1 Ferry Building #3, San Francisco, CA 94111

Phone: (415) 861-8032

18. Coi

Cuisine: Contemporary Californian

Why it's good: Fine dining with an emphasis on seasonality and sustainability, offering a sophisticated tasting menu.

Address: 373 Broadway, San Francisco, CA 94133

Phone: (415) 393-9000

19. Anchor Oyster Bar

Cuisine: Seafood

Why it's good: Cozy seafood spot known for its clam chowder, crab cakes, and fresh oysters.

Address: 579 Castro St, San Francisco, CA 94114

Phone: (415) 431-3990

20. Beretta

Cuisine: Italian

Why it's good: Trendy restaurant with a lively atmosphere, known for its delicious cocktails and wood-fired pizzas.

Address: 1199 Valencia St, San Francisco, CA 94110 **Phone**: (415) 695-1199

21. Zazie

Cuisine: French

Why it's good: Charming bistro offering French-inspired brunch and dinner dishes, with a lovely garden patio.

Address: 941 Cole St, San Francisco, CA 94117

Phone: (415) 564-5332

22. The Progress

Cuisine: Californian

Why it's good: Creative and seasonal menu served family-style in a stylish, contemporary setting.

Address: 1525 Fillmore St, San Francisco, CA 94115

Phone: (415) 673-1294

23. Michael Mina

Cuisine: Contemporary American

Why it's good: High-end dining with an innovative menu and impeccable service, offering a luxurious dining experience.

Address: 252 California St, San Francisco, CA 94111

Phone: (415) 397-9222

24. Sotto Mare

Cuisine: Italian/Seafood

Why it's good: Popular spot for classic Italian seafood dishes, including its famous cioppino.

Address: 552 Green St, San Francisco, CA 94133 **Phone**: (415) 398-3181

25. Frances

Cuisine: Californian

Why it's good: Intimate setting with a menu focusing on seasonal, locally sourced ingredients.

Address: 3870 17th St, San Francisco, CA 94114

Phone: (415) 621-3870

26. Tommaso's

Cuisine: Italian

Why it's good: Historic pizzeria known for its wood-fired pizzas and classic Italian dishes.

Address: 1042 Kearny St, San Francisco, CA 94133 **Phone**: (415) 398-9696

27. Cotogna

Cuisine: Italian

Why it's good: Rustic Italian fare with a focus on wood-fired cooking and house-made pasta.

Address: 490 Pacific Ave, San Francisco, CA 94133 **Phone**: (415) 775-8508

28. Octavia

Cuisine: Californian

Why it's good: Cozy and stylish restaurant with a menu highlighting seasonal ingredients and inventive dishes.

Address: 1701 Octavia St, San Francisco, CA 94109

Phone: (415) 408-7507

29. SPQR

Cuisine: Italian

Why it's good: Contemporary Italian cuisine with a focus on handmade pasta and creative, seasonal dishes.

Address: 1911 Fillmore St, San Francisco, CA 94115 **Phone**: (415) 771-7779

30. Marlowe

Cuisine: American

Why it's good: Known for its signature burger and American comfort food with a modern twist, served in a chic setting.

Address: 500 Brannan St, San Francisco, CA 94107

Phone: (415) 777-1413

10

Chapter 10. Where to Stay: Overnight Lodging

From lowest to highest price point. With addresses and phone numbers

1. San Francisco Downtown Hostel
  Cost: $50-$100 per night
  Address: 312 Mason St, San Francisco, CA 94102
  Phone: (415) 788-5604

2. Green Tortoise Hostel
  Cost: $50-$100 per night
  Address: 494 Broadway, San Francisco, CA 94133
  Phone: (415) 834-1000

3.Adelaide Hostel
  Cost: $60-$110 per night
  Address: 5 Isadora Duncan Ln, San Francisco, CA 94102
  Phone: (415) 359-1915

4.Europa Hotel

Cost: $70-$120 per night

Address: 310 Columbus Ave, San Francisco, CA 94133

Phone: (415) 391-5779

5.The Urban

Cost: $80-$130 per night

Address: 507 Bush St, San Francisco, CA 94108

Phone: (415) 432-7867

6.Pacific Motor Inn (Pacifica)

Cost: $80-$140 per night

Address: 200 Rockaway Beach Ave, Pacifica, CA 94044

Phone: (650) 359-7700

7.Grant Plaza Hotel

Cost: $90-$140 per night

Address: 465 Grant Ave, San Francisco, CA 94108

Phone: (415) 434-3883

8.SFO El Rancho Inn, SureStay Collection by Best Western (Millbrae)

Cost: $100-$150 per night

Address: 1100 El Camino Real, Millbrae, CA 94030

Phone: (650) 588-8500

9.Red Coach Motor Lodge

Cost: $110-$160 per night

Address: 700 Eddy St, San Francisco, CA 94109

Phone: (415) 474-5713

10.San Remo Hotel

Cost: $110-$160 per night
Address: 2237 Mason St, San Francisco, CA 94133
Phone: (415) 776-8688

11Hotel Beresford

Cost: $120-$170 per night
Address: 635 Sutter St, San Francisco, CA 94102
Phone: (415) 673-9900

12.Nob Hill Motor Inn

Cost: $120-$170 per night
Address: 1630 Pacific Ave, San Francisco, CA 94109
Phone: (415) 775-8160

13.Pacifica Motor Inn (Pacifica)

Cost: $120-$180 per night
Address: 200 Rockaway Beach Ave, Pacifica, CA 94044
Phone: (650) 359-7700

14.The Mosser

Cost: $130-$180 per night
Address: 54 4th St, San Francisco, CA 94103
Phone: (415) 986-4400

15.Coventry Motor Inn

Cost: $130-$180 per night
Address: 1901 Lombard St, San Francisco, CA 94123
Phone: (415) 567-1200

16.Comfort Inn by the Bay

Cost: $140-$190 per night

Address: 2775 Van Ness Ave, San Francisco, CA 94109
Phone: (415) 928-5000

17.Hotel Stratford
Cost: $140-$200 per night
Address: 242 Powell St, San Francisco, CA 94102
Phone: (415) 397-7080

18.Hotel Zephyr
Cost: $150-$220 per night
Address: 250 Beach St, San Francisco, CA 94133
Phone: (415) 392-6700

19.Columbus Motor Inn
Cost: $150-$220 per night
Address: 1075 Columbus Ave, San Francisco, CA 94133 **Phone: (415) 772-5000**
20.The Good Hotel
Cost: $150-$230 per night
Address: 112 7th St, San Francisco, CA 94103
Phone: (415) 621-7001

21.Holiday Inn San Francisco-Golden Gateway
Cost: $160-$240 per night
Address: 1500 Van Ness Ave, San Francisco, CA 94109
Phone: (415) 441-4000

22.Holiday Inn Express & Suites San Francisco Fishermans Wharf
Cost: $170-$250 per night
Address: 550 N Point St, San Francisco, CA 94133
Phone: (415) 409-4600

23.Hotel Zoe Fisherman's Wharf

Cost: $170-$250 per night
Address: 425 North Point St, San Francisco, CA 94133
Phone: (415) 561-1100

24.Handlery Union Square Hotel

Cost: $180-$260 per night
Address: 351 Geary St, San Francisco, CA 94102 **Phone**: (415) 781-7800

25.Marriott San Francisco Fisherman's Wharf

Cost: $190-$270 per night
Address: 1250 Columbus Ave, San Francisco, CA 94133
Phone: (415) 775-7555

26.Hotel Del Sol

Cost: $190-$270 per night
Address: 3100 Webster St, San Francisco, CA 94123
Phone: (415) 921-5520

27.The Marker San Francisco

Cost: $200-$290 per night
Address: 501 Geary St, San Francisco, CA 94102
Phone: (415) 292-0100

28.Hotel Nikko San Francisco

Cost: $220-$320 per night
Address: 222 Mason St, San Francisco, CA 94102
Phone: (415) 394-1111

29.Hyatt Regency San Francisco

Cost: $240-$350 per night
Address: 5 Embarcadero Center, San Francisco, CA 94111
Phone: (415) 788-1234
30.Fairmont San Francisco
Cost: $300-$450 per night
Address: 950 Mason St, San Francisco, CA 94108
Phone: (415) 772-5000

Chapter 11. Grocery Store Supermarkets

1. Safeway - Mission & 30th
   Address: 3350 Mission St, San Francisco, CA 94110 **Telephone:** (415) 824-1901

2. Whole Foods Market - SoMa
   Address: 399 4th St, San Francisco, CA 94107 **Telephone:** (415) 618-0066

3. Trader Joe's - Nob Hill
   Address: 1095 Hyde St, San Francisco, CA 94109 **Telephone:** (415) 474-1492

4. Safeway - Marina
   Address: 15 Marina Blvd, San Francisco, CA 94123 **Telephone:** (415) 563-4946

5. Whole Foods Market - Potrero Hill
   Address: 450 Rhode Island St, San Francisco, CA 94107 **Telephone:**

(415) 552-1155

6. Trader Joe's - SoMa
Address: 10 4th St, San Francisco, CA 94103 **Telephone:** (415) 536-7801

7. Safeway - Castro
Address: 2020 Market St, San Francisco, CA 94114 **Telephone:** (415) 861-7660

8. Whole Foods Market - Noe Valley
Address: 3950 24th St, San Francisco, CA 94114 **Telephone:** (415) 282-4700

9. Safeway - North Beach
Address: 350 Bay St, San Francisco, CA 94133 **Telephone:** (415) 885-1248

10. Trader Joe's - Stonestown
Address: 265 Winston Dr, San Francisco, CA 94132 **Telephone:** (415) 681-3181

12

Chapter 12. Telephone Numbers and Addresses You Should Know

Emergency Services:
Police, Fire, Medical Emergency: 911

Non-Emergency Services:
San Francisco Police Department (Non-Emergency): (415) 553-0123
San Francisco Fire Department (Non-Emergency): (415) 558-3200

Hospitals:
Zuckerberg San Francisco General Hospital and Trauma Center:
Address: 1001 Potrero Ave, San Francisco, CA 94110 **Telephone:** (628) 206-8000

UCSF Medical Center:
Address: 505 Parnassus Ave, San Francisco, CA 94143 **Telephone:** (415) 476-1000

California Pacific Medical Center (CPMC) – Van Ness Campus:

Address: 1101 Van Ness Ave, San Francisco, CA 94109 **Telephone:** (415) 600-6000

Saint Francis Memorial Hospital:

Address: 900 Hyde St, San Francisco, CA 94109
Telephone: (415) 353-6000

Rental Car Services:

Enterprise Rent-A-Car:

Address: 233 Ellis St, San Francisco, CA 94102 **Telephone:** (415) 837-1700

Hertz Car Rental:

Address: 325 Mason St, San Francisco, CA 94102 **Telephone:** (415) 771-0671

Budget Car Rental:

Address: 821 Howard St, San Francisco, CA 94103 **Telephone:** (415) 536-0660

Taxi Services:

Yellow Cab Co-op:

Telephone: (415) 333-3333

Luxor Cab:

Telephone: (415) 282-4141

Public Transportation:

San Francisco Municipal Transportation Agency (Muni):

Customer Service: (415) 701-2311

Bay Area Rapid Transit (BART):
  Customer Service: (510) 464-7134

Tourist Information:
  San Francisco Travel Association:
  Address: 749 Howard St, San Francisco, CA 94103 **Telephone:** (415) 391-2000
  Animal Control:
  San Francisco Animal Care & Control:
  Address: 1419 Bryant St, San Francisco, CA 94103 **Telephone:** (415) 554-6364

Poison Control:
  California Poison Control System:
  Telephone: 1-800-222-1222

13

Chapter 13. Security Precautions to be Aware of When Visiting San Francisco

San Francisco is a relatively safe place to visit for tourists, but you should be aware of becoming a target by any unscrupulous minded opportunist.

The crime rates in San Francisco vary by the neighborhood that are safe and those you should avoid.

I have made a list below consisting of: General Safety tips, type of crimes in San Francisco (and how to avoid them), Neighborhood areas to avoid, Homelessness, Health and Hygiene Considerations, and the San Francisco weather.

Lastly, the main thing to staying safe in San Francisco - or anywhere - is to always pay attention to what's going on around you.

General Safety Tips:

1. **Stay Alert:** Be aware of your surroundings, especially in crowded areas and tourist spots.
2. **Secure Belongings:** Keep personal items secure, as pickpocketing can be an issue in busy areas.

3. **Avoid Displaying Valuables:** Don't openly display expensive items like jewelry, cameras, and electronics.
4. **Use Trusted Transportation:** Stick to licensed taxis, ride-sharing services, and public transportation.
5. **Stay in Well-Lit Areas:** Avoid poorly lit streets and alleys, particularly at night.
6. **Be Cautious with ATMs:** Use ATMs located in well-lit, secure areas, and be aware of your surroundings while withdrawing cash.

Crime and Theft:

Pickpocketing and Theft: Common in crowded tourist areas like Fisherman's Wharf, Union Square, and on public transportation.

Car Break-Ins: Do not leave valuables visible in your car. Car break-ins can happen even in busy areas. Use a parking garage when possible.

Scams: Be cautious of individuals approaching you with suspicious offers or asking for money.

Areas to Be Cautious Of:

While San Francisco is generally safe, certain neighborhoods have higher crime rates. Exercise caution in the following areas:

Tenderloin: Known for higher rates of crime, including drug activity and theft. It's best to avoid walking alone at night in this area.

Civic Center: Similar to the Tenderloin, this area can be less safe, particularly after dark.

South of Market (SoMa): While this area has many attractions, parts of it can be less safe, especially at night.

Bayview-Hunters Point: This area has higher crime rates and is less frequented by tourists.

Health and Hygiene:

Public Restrooms: Public restrooms may not always be clean or safe. Use restrooms in cafes, restaurants, or hotels when possible.

Sanitation: San Francisco has made efforts to address homelessness and related sanitation issues, but be cautious and practice good hygiene, especially in downtown areas.

Homelessness:

Homeless Population: San Francisco has a significant homeless population. While most individuals are not dangerous, it's best to avoid confrontations and be cautious in areas with large homeless encampments.

Natural Precautions:

Weather: San Francisco's weather can be unpredictable. Dress in layers to be prepared for sudden changes.

Earthquakes: San Francisco is in an earthquake-prone area. Familiarize yourself with earthquake safety measures, such as knowing the nearest exits and safe spots.

14

Resources:

Inside Guide to San Francisco Tourism. (n.d.). *San Francisco crime.* Inside Guide to San Francisco Tourism. Retrieved July 6, 2024, from https://www.inside-guide-to-san-francisco-tourism.com/san-franci sco-crime.html

San Francisco Recreation and Parks. (n.d.). *Golden Gate Park points of interest.* https://sfrecpark.org/1116/Golden-Gate-Park-Points-of-Interest

Free Tours by Foot. (2024, July 6). *San Francisco at night.* https://free toursbyfoot.com/san-francisco-at-night/

U.S. News & World Report. (n.d.). *Things to do in San Francisco, CA.* https://travel.usnews.com/San_Francisco_CA/Things_To_Do/ .

49 Miles. (2022). *A brief history of San Francisco: Everything you need to know.* https://49miles.com/2022/a-brief-history-of-san-francisco-everything-you-need-to-know/

A Passion and A Passport. (n.d.). *Hidden gems in San Francisco.* https://apassionandapassport.com/hidden-gems-in-san-francisco/

Hotels.com. (n.d.). *Best beaches in San Francisco.* https://www.hotels. com/go/usa/us-best-beaches-san-francisco

The New York Times. (n.d.). *Best San Francisco restaurants.* https://w

ww.nytimes.com/article/best-san-francisco-restaurants.html

San Francisco Travel Association. (n.d.). *Top 20 attractions in San Francisco.* https://www.sftravel.com/article/top-20-attractions-san-francisco

Inside Guide to San Francisco Tourism. (n.d.). *Haight-Ashbury.* https://www.inside-guide-to-san-francisco-tourism.com/haight-ashbury.html

Made in the USA
Columbia, SC
15 July 2024

38660655R10067